Old BOTHWELL

by
Rhona Wilson

We don't know anything about this picture except that it was taken in Bothwellhaugh *c.*1924, and that the ice-cream vendor was called Tony.

First Published in the United Kingdom, 1997
By Stenlake Publishing, Ochiltree Sawmill, The Lade,
Ochiltree, Ayrshire KA18 2NX
Tel/Fax: 01290 423114

ISBN 1 872074 97 9

Kirkfield Church was at the Uddingston end of Main Street opposite the entrance to Bothwell Castle golf course. It was built in 1860, and prior to that its members met in a school in Uddingston and at Wooddean Church. The two churches were amalgamated in the early forties, eventually uniting with St Brides to form Bothwell Parish Church in 1976. Since then both Kirkfield and Wooddean have been demolished and flats built in their place.

Introduction

Pretty as it may be, it is difficult to see Bothwell as a holiday resort, harder still as a hotbed of political violence. Both these unlikely distinctions, however, feature strongly in its past.

It was Walter de Moravia, thirteenth century owner, who built its original castle, restored later by the infamous Archibald The Grim who founded St Bride's Collegiate Church on what later became Main Street. The village's name, by turns 'Botheville', 'Bothwel' and 'Bothell', was first referred to in its present form in a charter to the Countess of Angus in 1581. Its derivation comes from the combination of the Celtic 'both' meaning dwelling and 'ael' or 'ayl' meaning river giving 'dwelling beside the river'.

After the Reformation John Hamilton, previously prior of Blantyre Priory, merrily swapped religion to become the first minister of Bothwell parish. He obviously wasn't the man of principle that Bothwell's Covenanters were. In the seventeenth century hoards of Scots signed the National Covenant declaring their loyalty to the state but their wish for free religious choice after various monarchs tried to impose episcopacy on the Scottish Church. Thousands died in the ensuing years, and the Battle of Bothwell Bridge was infamous as a Covenanting failure. Outnumbered three to one and disorganised to boot, they didn't stand a chance, although Presbyterianism was restored to Scotland by William of Orange just nine years afterwards.

Agriculture was Bothwell's staple employment for centuries, supplemented by weaving. The village had particularly fertile soil and as well as having its own Fair Day was physically close to the markets of Hamilton, Airdrie and Glasgow. In the 1790s its contract weavers were supplied with raw materials by Glasgow manufacturers, paid a piece rate per garment. Bothwell's population started to rise in the late eighteenth century quite simply because improved agricultural methods meant increased food supplies. Even so, famine was a possibility as late as 1801. In this year Bothwell's minister withdrew his annual stipend in meal to distribute to his starving parishioners.

During the early nineteenth century Bothwell developed not because of the Industrial Revolution but as an antidote to it. In the 1790s there were a mere fifty colliers in the parish as a whole and, with its fresh climate, the village came to be seen as an oasis for jaded industrialists. Businessmen filled in Bothwell's wide, open spaces with sandstone residences whilst the Clyde Hotel, built in Main Street in 1860, catered for the summer tourists. They must have been shocked, then, by the dramatic changes of the 1870s. Previously undiscovered coal was found in the village during a survey in the 1850s and two decades later Baird and Co. decided to capitalise on it by sinking Castle Pit just off Main Street.

Coal-mining changed the village considerably. The North British Railway arrived in 1878 to link the pit to Glasgow and was joined soon after by another station just across the road on Main Street. Miners' tenements sprung up to join the sandstone villas and house the influx of workers. Although some may have argued the village was ruined it was from this point onwards that Bothwell's facilities developed, broadening its potential for recreation and education. A library appeared in the 1870s, joined within the next decade by a primary school and the public halls. Castle Pit became the village's industrial focal point for the next few decades.

Despite predictions that Bothwell's coal would last until the 1960s the mine closed after subsidence in the shaft in the fifties. The village's agricultural tradition was also failing and in 1951 only 355 of its 3,000 strong population found work within Bothwell. Today most employment is service-based, supplied by shops and hotels which benefit from the visitors who still flock in. In the end Bothwell's pretty face has been its fortune, its good looks standing it in far greater stead than its industrial past. Well kept streets and upmarket shops and cafes testify to a healthy middle class population.

Old Bothwell Castle was built from local red sandstone in the thirteenth century, and considering its history its surprising there's any of it left. By the fourteenth century it had already been dismantled twice. After the Battle of Bannockburn, Robert Bruce ordered its destruction as part of a 'scorched earth' tactic which demanded the wreck of property reclaimed from the English, thereby making sure there was nothing for them to steal in future. During the mid-eighteenth century the Bothwell estate was subjected to a very different kind of threat at the hands of the mighty Hamiltons. In the 1760s the Duke of Douglas died childless and his sister, living in Paris, inherited Bothwell Estate. Attempts to pass this on to her son resulted in a huge lawsuit by the Duke of Hamilton who had designs on the estate and claimed that the boy had been bought and was not a rightful heir. The Douglas family won the drawn-out case after an appeal in 1769.

By the seventeenth century the trend for fortress-like mansion houses had waned and Bothwell Castle's then owner, the First Earl of Forfar, decided he would like a more modern home. Around 1670 he began to plunder the old castle to build a new mansion house (above). Unlike the usual castle legends of secret passages and ghosts that were attributed to the original building, stories relating to the Earl's new home were suitably modern. Bizzarely, the building's demise was blamed on the misguided zeal of some Belgian nuns. Billeted there as refugees during the First World War, their obsessive floor-scrubbing apparently speeded up the mansion's bad case of dry rot, although at four centuries old the floors were probably somewhat the worse for wear anyway. By 1926 the castle was considered beyond repair and demolished.

This quaint dwelling in the grounds of Bothwell Castle was built in the late eighteenth century and used as a pit-stop by out-of-puff aristocrats enjoying a stroll. For years it was known mistakenly by locals as Queen Mary's Cottage. Although Mary Queen of Scots married an Earl of Bothwell they never stayed at Bothwell Castle, and would surely have found more luxurious accommodation than this humble abode. As with the numerous Queen Mary Rooms and Views in castles en route to the Battle of Langside, the link is tenuous to say the least. Having become an attraction to local vandals, the dilapidated cottage was razed to the ground on the orders of the Earl of Home in 1936.

These Woodlands Crescent homes were built during the inter-war years as part of the 'Homes for Heroes' scheme. During the Second World War morale-raising projects went into full swing in Bothwell, with people being urged to clear out their attics to guard against fires and to take part in the 'Dig for Victory' campaign. This latter exercise involved people growing their own vegetables to be as self-sufficient as possible and have fresh veg all year round. Many public parks across Britain were temporarily turned into allotments in the process.

There was a private railway in the north-east of Bothwell Parish prior to 1800. This linked two collieries to the wharves of the Monkland Canal, and significantly predated the first public line in the area, the Wishaw and Coltness Railway, which opened a station at Holytown (now Mossend) in 1833. By the early 1840s a passenger service was running between Glasgow and Newarthill, with a Caledonian Railway service from Glasgow to Carlisle in operation soon afterwards. *C*.1876 the Bothwell - Hamilton branch line was introduced to connect to the Glasgow - Carlise service.

This viaduct formed part of Bothwell's railway link to Blantyre and Hamilton, and fell into disrepair when the line closed in the 1950s. The arrival of the railway coincided with industrialisation in the area and the beginning of serious pollution of the Clyde. Steamboats, the Glasgow fisheries and the Turkey Red factory at Blantyre all contributed to the demise of the river's once plentiful salmon stock. A dam built between Blantyre Mill and Bothwell was particularly damaging, preventing the fish from progressing upstream during their spawning season.

Castle Pit, off Station Road, was still operational when this picture was taken in the late forties. When it opened seventy years earlier it not only changed the landscape by springing up slap bang in the middle of the village, but also prompted the arrival of the North British railway line and its accompanying viaduct. With increasing industrialisation, Bothwell's population grew from *c*.470 in the 1790s to over 3,000 a century later. The village was used to incomers in the form of holiday-makers or rich commuters but didn't take so kindly to the influx of miners, many of them Irish immigrants. To keep workers out of view as they walked to and from work a tunnel was built from the miners' tenements in Fallside Road under Main Street - a very extreme tourist-pleasing measure.

Writing in the late eighteenth century, the author of Bothwell parish's first statistical account estimated that there were about 3,000 years' worth of coal reserves left in the area. This estimate was based on the prevailing extraction technology and market at the time. In the 1940s, the National Coal Board revised the forecast of the Castle Pit's reserves, giving it until around 1963. It is possible that there would have been coal left to mine after this date, but falling prices would have made it uneconomic to retrieve.

Although the Castle was pegged for closure in the early sixties its demise came far quicker. The mine was plagued by flooding, and when the shaft collapsed and made the pit unworkable it closed abruptly in 1950. Within the next year both of Bothwell's railway stations shut, and the village slowly reverted to its pre-mining state. In the meantime it had to contend with the eyesores left by the former industry. The abandoned LMS station on Main Street was as much a blot on the landscape as the derelict pit, pictured here in all its wasteland glory after closure.

On the 1869 Ordnance Survey map of Bothwell, Fallside Road appears as an unnamed country road through Whitley's Loan. Asides from Longdale Lunatic Asylum, which stood roughly opposite where Kirkland's Hospital is now and a safe distance from Main Street, there were no other buildings on the road except a cottage at Kirklands. This changed dramatically when Fallside Road was chosen by Baird and Sons, Castle Pit proprietors, to house their workers. Large tenement blocks including Waverley Place and Castle Square were put up, and a Miner's Welfare Institute for dances and meetings appeared some time later. In later life the Institute was sold to the Catholic church and used for worship until the RC church was built in the early seventies. This picture, looking towards Main Street, shows Waverley Place, now the site of a low-rise housing development called Waverley Court.

Castle Square was put up in 1898 and quickly earned the nickname 'Jubilee' since it was built on the fiftieth anniversary of Queen Victoria's accession to the throne. It was made up of two rows with communal washhouses in the middle. When the square was built few homes had an indoor bath and cleanliness required either a free standing tub, a session at the kitchen sink, or a trip to the close washhouse - there was of course the option not to bother. In reality most people booked into the washhouse rota, which could be shared by several stairs' worth of tenants and was strictly regimented. It seems astonishing that although miners did a grimy job pit owners seldom bothered to supply pithead baths. Bothwellhaugh, for example, didn't get its baths till the miner's welfare installed some in the fifties; by that time the 'Pallis' mine was on its deathbed.

Today this section of Fallside Road is recognisable only by the low stone wall. Although Bothwell residents pushed for a village conservation order it seems that some Victorian tenements were more dispensable than others. All of Fallside Road's miners' tenements were demolished in the seventies, and it might appear that the village wanted to wipe out every last reminder of the mining industry which hijacked it. To be fair, at the time of the demolitions the country was in the grip of an obsession with the modern. Anything old was considered to be outmoded and anything new - shopping centres and tower blocks - was wonderful. Councils everywhere were dispensing with old buildings like an outdated wardrobe and looking at the state of these Fallside tenements there seems little incentive to preserve them. It wasn't till the mid to late seventies that conservation became an issue by which time Fallside Road had well and truly missed the boat.

Bothwell Parish Church is actually two buildings joined at the tower. The section on the right was originally the Collegiate Church of St Brides, founded in the late fourteenth century by Archibald the Grim. Legend has it that he built it to appease his conscience after a particularly horrendous crime (he committed many) and decided its location on the outcome of an arrow-shooting competition. Collegiate churches were strange fish incorporating a league of clergymen (known as prebendaries) with a Provost as president, all gathered in one location. This meant that ministers for Strathaven, say, lived in a manse in Bothwell for most of the year. St Brides fell into disrepair in the late 1820s and a replacement was built beside it in 1833. Both churches remained separate until 100 years later when architect J. Jeffrey Waddell had a master-stroke, designing the central tower to unite them and creating a building which is still the stunning centrepiece of the village.

Right: A twelfth century grave slab at Bothwell Parish Church, possibly belonging to the ancient Olifard family. In 1825 Robert Owen founded a co-operative community called the Orbiston Experiment with the aim of reducing poor rates and abolishing pauperism. Two hundred people moved into the premises near Bellshill, with Bothwell's minister sniping that they were 'certainly not the elite of their respective countries'. His parishioners agreed, referring to the commune as 'Babylon' and seeming to consider it a dangerous subversion of 'normal' values. The minister couldn't hide his satisfaction when the venture failed because of financial mismanagement. He allowed himself a footnote in his statistical account of Bothwell to say that when the parish church became dilapidated he gave his sermons instead in the abandoned Babylon buildings, obviously enjoying the delicious irony of it all.

Above: During the 1933 renovation workers uncovered remains of an even earlier Norman church on site. Two monumental stones were discovered including the grave slab pictured here. The three stars represent the Moray Arms and the sword a warrior. It is thought to be the gravestone of Walter de Moravia (Moray), thirteenth century builder of Bothwell, and local tradition likes to think that Walter and his spouse are buried near the east wing of the church.

The writer Joanna Baillie, daughter of a Bothwell minister, was born in 1762. The family moved frequently because of Dr Baillie's career (he wasn't always popular in the village) and she left Bothwell aged seven. Around twenty years later she was living in London and had published her first work, *Fugitive Verses*. She fell in with Wordsworth and Scott, Byron himself commenting graciously that she was 'the only woman who could write a tragedy'. The whimsical verses she wrote comparing the weavers' cottages in Bothwell's Green Street to fairy bowers testify to her middle class background, jarringly out of touch with working class reality. The churchyard monument pictured here was erected by James Donald in the 1890s, several decades after her death. Its beautiful mosaic panels were hand-made in Venice and are intact to this day.

Bothwell Main Street, 1937. The left-hand side of the street has changed massively with all the buildings before the church demolished. While the frontage of the Caledonian Railway Station has been demolished, the platform buildings remain as part of the Edgecumbe Instruments factory.

Bothwell's Public Halls were opened in 1888, a decade after the Castle Pit arrived and the village population soared. They didn't make their century, being demolished in the early 1970s along with various tenement blocks.

Part of the Belmos factory, Main Street. When the old Caley station closed in the early fifties it lay abandoned for several years. Local businessman, Tom Coughtrie of Fairfield Lodge, bought the premises in 1956 for the Belmos Engineering Company he had set up in Bellshill. It opened after conversion, and was a much needed boost to the local economy at the time.

With strong fertile soil, better than that of the rest of the parish, Bothwell was originally an agricultural community. A variety of crops were sown, with wheat becoming popular in the late eighteenth century since it could be grown on fields which previously had to be left fallow. Potatoes were grown by almost every farmer for their own food and fodder needs. Wilkie's Plough, invented up the road in Uddingston, was used from the turn of the nineteenth century because it required fewer animals to power it. Situated close to Glasgow, Hamilton and Airdrie, Bothwell was well-placed for the surrounding markets although its farming origins haven't survived the twentieth century. While seven farms made it into the 1900s there are none at the present time, the last market gardens also closing in the 1970s.

Bothwell, with its classy boutiques, has been fashion conscious for over 200 years. The author of Bothwell's First Statistical Account commented that his parishioners' dress had improved dramatically over the 1770 to 1790 period. He attributed workers' demands for higher wages to this increasing fashion consciousness, and didn't seem to approve. Over the nineteenth century women's clothing in particular became more and more extravagant. The culmination of this, the bustle, arrived some time after David Livingstone began to open up Africa. Reports began to circulate on the beautiful Namibian women, focusing on their large bottoms which one commentator described as 'like a delicious shelf jutting out behind'. British fashion took up the mantle, eventually developing the voluptuous bustle which gathered up layers of cloth into a pert mound at the back of a dress.

Weaving, another of Bothwell's long lost industries, was a staple occupation in the village at the turn of the nineteenth century, although things went into a decline soon afterwards. Bothwell weavers joined the fourteen week strike of 1811 which failed miserably, resulting in them accepting lower rates for their work. In 1815 Bonaparte was defeated and the village celebrated along with the rest of the country. It is doubtful whether the villagers would have been quite so enthusiastic if they could have foreseen the unemployment the end of the Napoleonic Wars would bring. The handloom weavers benefited from a large amount of weaving work in the form of war goods, and they suffered considerably once this was gone. Bothwell Mill didn't help matters when it opened with ninety powerlooms, but this got its come-uppance in turn. The massive Blantyre Mills totally usurped it when they opened in the late eighteenth century.

The Glasgow, Bothwell, Hamilton and Wishaw Tramways Act authorised the construction of a tramway route through the parish in 1872. Thereafter absolutely nothing was done, and the issue disappeared until Hamilton Town Council decided to organise it themselves towards the end of the century. The council approached interested local authorities and it was decided to build a Blantyre/Wishaw tramway, with construction beginning in 1902. A year later 30,000 people turned up to see the hurlies on their first day. Bothwell didn't get its own trams till 1910, and they had a short renaissance, only offering a limited service during World War I after which they were hit by stiff competition from motor buses. In 1925 the tramway company was reduced to buying buses to keep up. The service was downgraded in the thirties, and the Bothwell rails were lifted in 1932.

The 1869 Ordnance Survey map shows a very different Bothwell from this picture. Westport, where the original village gates would have been, is situated off Main Street near the subsequent site of Castle Pit. The Blantyre works are across the river with a suspension bridge for workers travelling to them. Overall Bothwell is shown as a small and scattered community, with most buildings situated in Main Street around the church, and a row of dwellings around the Free Church further up the road.

Most of the buildings in this turn of the century shot of Main Street are intact but it still presents a very different picture today. The fountain is no longer there, removed when it became too much of an obstruction to the increasingly popular motor car. Despite getting a motorway bypass some time ago Bothwell Main Street is still extremely busy. Any horse and carts or dogs loitering in the middle of it today would be flattened in seconds.

The same corner a couple of decades later. Motorbuses scattered down the road in this 1930s picture show that Bothwell's trams have been and gone. The first shop jutting out on the left belonged to the Fotheringhams from the late fifties. Previous to this it had been a baby linen shop, empty for some time before they took it over. They considered their options and eventually turned it into an ironmongers called Minto House (the Mintos were the original owners of the building) because their own name was such a mouthful. Christmas used to start in Bothwell when the Fotheringhams put their Christmas tree out on the roof of their shop. Just down from Minto House was Tunnocks, now a hairdressers.

The Donald Institute adjoins Bothwell Public School and was opened in 1910, offering reading and recreation rooms. Its benefactor was James Donald, a Glasgow chemical manufacturer who left money to finance the institute, which also acted as a memorial to him. Recreation institutes were considered to be a useful instrument for improving community life by acting as a distraction to the pub, and Bothwell's was of course run on strict temperance principles. In later years it was lucky enough to be taken over as the public library - lucky, because philanthropists such as Donald often didn't leave enough money in their wills to maintain their memorial buildings and many fell apart through disrepair. Incidentally, Bothwell's first public subscription library was slated by a nineteenth century minister for its immoral book choice.

Silverwells runs off Main Street and is pretty much intact although its shops have changed - it now holds a Chinese restaurant and a gun shop. Thomson's butcher is marked in this picture by the canopy on the left. There was originally a malt kiln in Silverwells and afterwards a weaving establishment with an atrocious reputation regarding crime. Bothwell's local plan of the early 1980s touted Silverwells as a good example of local heritage, commenting that east Main Street had been similarly well preserved until some unfortunate housing developments were approved.

By 1899 the map of Bothwell shows considerable development. The pit and railways have sprung up and there are more churches for the village's larger population. A viaduct has appeared for the North British Railway which runs under The Crescent. Craighead has a colliery, as have many other small-holdings such as Whistleberry. The colliery rows at Fallside have appeared and both sides of The Crescent (later Silverwells Crescent) have been developed. Mill Road has graduated into a proper road instead of a track, and St. Andrew's Avenue and Fife Crescent have been created.

Silvertrees Hotel, Silverwells, was originally Braidenhill House, one of the largest residences in Bothwell. It belonged to JB Tennant who owned the steel works in Whifflet, Coatbridge. If you walk into Sivertrees foyer today and look up, you'll see the initials of him and his wife embossed in gold on the ceiling.

Mention is made of Bothwell Bridge in repair records of the 1640s, although it may have been built by Archibald the Grim as early as 1400. Prior to 1650 the crossing was hugely important since there were no other bridges over the Clyde before Glasgow, while in the 1780s the Glasgow-Carlisle coach route used it. Once a twelve foot wide hump-backed structure complete with a gatehouse in the middle to collect tolls, the bridge has since been straightened, widened and surrounded by motorways. A few miles down the Calder there is a cave which was supposedly one of William Wallace's many hiding places.

The background to the Covenanting disputes of the seventeenth century is chaotic to say the least. James VI of Scotland set the ball rolling when he also became King of England and tried to impose episcopacy (government by a system of bishops) on the Scottish Church. Despite the unpopularity of the policy, successive sovereigns continued to try and adopt it. By 1638 things had got so bad that thousands of Scots took the step of signing the National Covenant which declared loyalty to the crown but asserted the principle of religious freedom. In the 1660s there was another attempt to impose Espicopacy which led to a period of Civil War including the Battle of Bothwell Bridge. William of Orange eventually restored Scottish Presbyterianism in the late 1680s but the victory was slow in coming, taking twenty-eight years of fighting and the deaths of 18,000 Covenanters.

The Battle of Bothwell Bridge in 1679 was a disastrous defeat for the Covenanters, coming as it did after their victory at Drumlog a few weeks earlier. Initially they didn't even expect to fight, having been informed that the Duke of Monmouth was to proceed peacefully. They also reckoned without the presence of Claverhouse, still smarting from his Drumclog defeat and eager to get his revenge. Only 300 Covenanters defended the bridge and when this gave way the army had a clear route to the rest assembled on the south side. They dispersed into small, squabbling groups and, without a clear lead, didn't stand a chance against the King's cavalry and cannon-fire. 400 were killed and 1,200 captured. Some of those who fled were protected by the Duchess of Hamilton who refused permission for Monmouth to search her estate.

Of those who were captured during the battle some were executed while others renounced their beliefs. Another unlucky group were sent off to American plantations in a ship which sunk. In the 1980s there was confusion over the status of the battle field which was owned by a trust. Commemorative services were held on it periodically but there was no official recognition of its status and there were fears that it was not protected from developers. A monument was erected for the Covenanters in 1903 and is still standing, although there has been talk of moving it to somewhere with more space. The brig's Lido, pictured here in 1950, was considered very fashionable at the time. Today the surrounding area has been developed as the Clyde Walkway, running through the village to Bothwell Castle and Uddingston.

Properties like Craighead House, set in an isolated position across the Bothwell Bridge, were once home to well-established families and successful industrialists. However, as fortunes and fashions changed during the first half of the twentieth century many were abandoned, falling into disrepair before finally being demolished. Some were sold off to make way for housing developments, while others underwent more eccentric reinventions. Calderpark, for example, became a zoo and Daldowie was transformed into a crematorium, while others became hospitals after temporary conversion during one of the world wars. For some reason several were converted into religious centres and this is what happened to Craighead. The Society of Jesus took over around 1916 and is still offering retreats to this day.

Bothwell's convent, situated near the bowling green, was opened as a private boarding school for girls by Franciscan nuns in the early 1870s. During the First World War it was awarded grant aid from the Scottish Education Department and started to take in day girls, becoming Elmwood Secondary School later in its career. The convent closed in the late 1970s and was converted into flats.

Three generations of the MacMillan family photographed at Silverhill on the old Bothwell Road, 1927. The property was previously a coaching inn known as Mary Steele's Inn. When this picture was taken Silverhill was a small dairy farm, with milk from the six Ayrshire cows sold in the village. Elizabeth MacMillan is on the left, accompanied by her granddaughter Georgina MacMillan Young and her great grandson William.

In the 1570s James Hamilton of Bothwellhaugh shot the Regent Murray dead in Linlithgow, a political move designed to benefit Mary Queen of Scots and, most likely, his own ambitious family. Until the late nineteenth century, Bothwellhaugh's tiny dairy farming community was known only for this bloody incident. Having bought mineral rights in the area, the Bent Colliery Company started mining Bothwellhaugh in 1884, spurred on by the high price of coal and technological developments which made the 'black gold' easier to access. The company was responsible for the development of the village. Officially called Hamilton Palace, the colliery was quickly nicknamed 'the Pallis'. Despite being only two miles from Bothwell this insular, mining-centred community could have been another planet.

Raith Place, 1963. Bothwellhaugh coal was of high quality and much sought after for industrial uses, particularly as fuel for steam trains. Much of it was exported to Argentinian railway companies, and the Flying Scot's record run to London was said to have used Pallis coal. The colliery's initial crew of just fourteen miners was quickly swollen by an influx of employees when its two pits were sunk in 1886. They needed accommodation and Bent built the Pallis tenements, first around the pithead and later out towards the Clyde. The two-storey buildings were of reasonable quality and modern for the time, but their allocation was not always fair. Stewart Thomson, pit cashier, also wielded the power of house allocation and according to villagers gave the biggest and best houses to non-union men. Pallis workers had to wait until the thirties for a points system which made housing provision more judicious.

Members of the Mining Institute of Scotland at Hamilton Palace Colliery 1899, cutting a very different figure from the men who worked the coal faces. Around 1914 the Pallis was churning out 2,000 tons of coal per day and with over 1,000 miners was the third biggest employer in Lanarkshire. Pallis miners participated in the national strikes of 1921 and 1926, and during the latter demonstration essential safety workers exempt from action were sacked when they refused to transport coal. All hell broke loose, and the following morning a mob of 500 gathered on a day which ended with seven miners being charged with violent picketing. The local union broke up after this unsuccessful strike, leaving the Pallis bereft of union support until the thirties. When the militant United Mineworkers of Scotland began to earn support in the village the coal company ran scared and asked the Lanarkshire Miner's Union to re-form as a moderate alternative.

Bothwellhaugh was mined until the fifties but, like other collieries, its decline began several decades earlier, aggravated by strikes and the depression. During the 1920s the Hamiltons (recipients of royalties from several pits including the Pallis) decided to allow mining under their palace and mausoleum, sacrificing their family heritage to subsidence. The Pallis community also found that their surroundings were being treated with little respect. Their tenement homes fell into disrepair and, particularly by the thirties, colliery conditions were deteriorating. Rail-lines for haulage were apparently almost worn out and both pits were vulnerable to flooding. Still, the mines enjoyed a revival of sorts after nationalisation. James Cowan, then manager, discovered several new areas of workable coal although this couldn't postpone Bothwellhaugh's fate indefinitely.

Bothwellhaugh's company school was taken over and extended by Bothwell School Board around the turn of the century. Its ornate brickwork was reflected in many Pallis buildings, particularly the pit office which was emblazoned with the date '1884' in white brick. With 500 pupils the school roll was at its highest during the First World War, dwindling to a stark ten in the mid-sixties. The overcrowding of the war years couldn't have helped in an environment scarcely conducive to study. The school was built in the shadow of the bing and pupils and teachers alike had to contend with the noise of the pithead. Bothwellhaugh's already distracted pupils must have wondered just what they were studying for - a glance out the window showed their future in plain view.

Co-ops began to emerge in the early nineteenth century when there was a period of severe recession. They provided a way for poor people to buy food cheaply, saving money into the bargain with the payment of annual dividends worth as much as ten weeks' wages. Collective ownership became increasingly relevant throughout the nineteenth century as numerous mining villages sprung up often with only one 'truck' shop, owned by the company and often charging exorbitant prices. Bothwellhaugh's Co-op opened in 1886 and paid particularly generous dividends. By the early sixties it had fallen into a dilapidated state.

Bothwellhaugh's Pipe Band. The Pallis was just one of countless mines that struggled through the first half of the twentieth century, although Bothwellhaugh's ultimate fate was unique. Its own sewage, of all things, brought about its downfall. The area was vulnerable to flooding and sewage pipes leading into the Clyde were badly designed, allowing backflow into the lower reaches of the village. Colliery owners seem to have been plagued by a short-term mentality, and considered that the problem was not worth fixing since the mine's working life was limited. By 1948 the health hazard was so great that a closure order was put on the village even though there was still coal left to mine. Affected Pallis workers were rehoused, and the colliery survived until 1959 when the Coal Board shut it because of flooding at Pit 2.

By 1960 most of Bothwellhaugh's miners' rows were empty. Five years later the area was derelict and suffering from massive subsidence; it remained abandoned until work started on Strathclyde Country Park (under development in this picture) in the early seventies. Strathclyde's new motorway routes ran right through the Bothwellhaugh area, which wasn't a pretty sight after five years of neglect. Despite being a good example of period architecture it was decided to demolish the village, the site of which now lies partly under the park's man-made loch. Although Bothwellhaugh became a veritable Atlantis, there is a residents' committee to this day, giving some idea of the strong sense of identity this isolated community had. The fact that the Pallis became the site of a huge community parkland is heartening, although the recent decision to build a shopping complex within it doesn't exactly inspire confidence.

Tom Gallagher, milkman, on his rounds at Bothwellhaugh.

Colliers had a reputation for pursuits such as drinking or gambling, although their managers preferred a sober workforce (in both senses of the word) and were quick to promote good, clean fun in the form of sport or group activities. Bothwellhaugh's bowling club must have scored on both counts, although I have come across some dated commentators who put bowling on a par with alcohol abuse because it meant that people were away from their homes. As well as joining in with the sports, clubs and bands Pallis workers also partook in whippet and pigeon racing. One miner returning from the annual summer trip was surprised to be congratulated on a race his dog had won since he thought it was in its kennel. Some of his workmates had taken the liberty of using the dog to win a few bob for themselves in his absence.

Palace United football team. There wasn't much chance of getting drunk in Bothwellhaugh since the village was dry until the 1950s, and those in search of a drink had to either walk to pubs in surrounding villages, such as the Douglas Arms in Bothwell, or get embroiled in the local football rivalries. Football was phenomenally popular at the turn of the century. Almost every street in larger towns had its own team and the Pallis was no exception. Before the company provided a football pitch near the public park teams played on the drying greens in front of Raith Place. Palace Rangers played on the new pitch until the land was taken over for colliery use around the time of the First World War. The second pitch was across the railway.

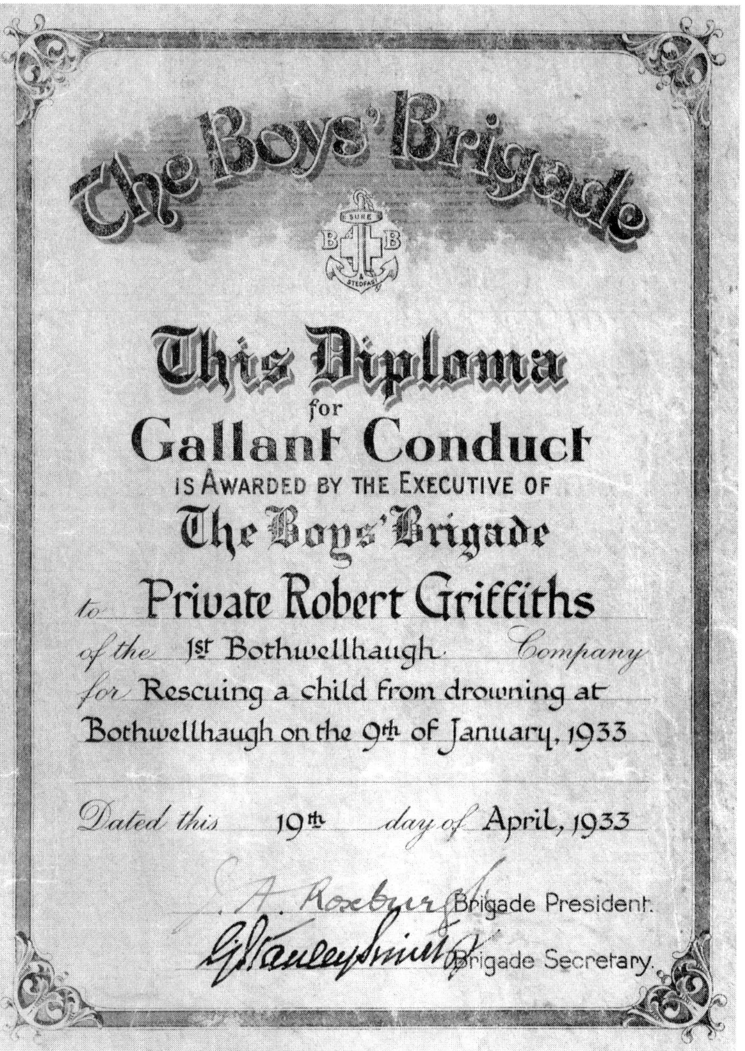

The Boys' Brigade

SURE & STEDFAST

This Diploma for Gallant Conduct is awarded by the Executive of The Boys' Brigade

to Private Robert Griffiths

of the 1st Bothwellhaugh Company

for Rescuing a child from drowning at Bothwellhaugh on the 9th of January, 1933

Dated this 19th day of April, 1933

Brigade President.

Brigade Secretary.

Victor Butler, Sam Butler and Tom Vance, 1930. This seemingly carefree picture was taken during the depression. The owner of Orbiston House took an interest in the miners of Bothwellhaugh and set up a boxing club to raise spirits; other activities were provided by the local Boys' Brigade company.

The best thing about Blantyre used to be this suspension bridge to Bothwell! An elderly gentleman collected the toll of 1*d*. from anyone who passed by his toll booth (on the near side of the bridge).